fresh, fast & fun QUILTS

Contents

What fun! Here are five amazing quilts to help you show off tempting textiles! Ann D. Hansen shares how simple it is to frame your favorite fabrics in the blocks of *Bohemian Babe* and *Jeweled Skylights.* Because it's so nice to have options, you'll see *Madison Avenue* and *Josie's Quilt* in two different colorways. Does *Gypsy Caravan* seem challenging to sew? It isn't! In fact, it's a snap with Snowball blocks—their clever color arrangement makes this easy design appear far more complex than it is. With Ann's exciting quilts, you've got fast and fashionable ways to make modern fabrics shine!

To complete your library of easy, energetic quilt patterns by Ann D. Hansen, get your copy of Leisure Arts book #5588 Make It Modern Quilts *at your local retailer or LeisureArts.com.*

Meet Ann D. Hansen

Ann D. Hansen loves color, even when she's not quilting. To relax, she enjoys decorating her Salt Lake City home. "Decorating lets me play with fabrics and colors in another way," Ann says. "My husband and I joke that the house is getting smaller inside because I've repainted the walls so many times."

"My maternal grandmother was a quilter," says Ann. "I didn't want to see the art lost in my family so I decided to learn. My daughter is in her third year of college, and she's slowly beginning to show an interest in quilting." Ann has done far more than just learn to quilt. She now has a pattern design company called Pixie Girl Quilts.

Ann says, "I love taking fabrics and seeing what I can create. Sometimes fabric inspires my designs. Other times, it's things I see—tiles in a floor or slats in a fence—or ideas just come to me at odd times. I always have graph paper handy. I hand draw all my designs."

You can see more of Ann's fun and lively designs at PixieGirlQuilts.com.

LEISURE ARTS, INC.
Little Rock, Arkansas

bohemian babe

Finished Quilt Size: 69" x 69" (175 cm x 175 cm)
Finished Block Size: 12" x 12" (30 cm x 30 cm)

Fabric Requirements

Yardage is based on 43"/44" (109 cm/112 cm) wide fabric with a usable width of 40" (102 cm).

- $^{1}/_{2}$ yd (46 cm) ***each*** of 12 assorted print fabrics
- $^{1}/_{2}$ yd (46 cm) ***each*** of 12 assorted tone-on-tone and/or solid color fabrics
- $^{5}/_{8}$ yd (57 cm) of fabric for binding
- $4^{3}/_{8}$ yds (4 m) of fabric for backing

You will also need:

- 77" x 77" (196 cm x 196 cm) piece of batting

Cutting

*Follow **Rotary Cutting**, page 39, to cut fabric. Cut all strips from the selvage-to-selvage width of the fabric. All measurements include $\frac{1}{4}$" seam allowances.*

From **each** print fabric:

- Cut 1 square $12\frac{5}{8}$" x $12\frac{5}{8}$". Cut square in half *twice* diagonally to make 4 **triangles.***
- Cut 2 **squares** $8\frac{1}{2}$" x $8\frac{1}{2}$".

From **each** assorted tone-on-tone or solid color fabric:

- Cut 5 strips $2\frac{1}{2}$" wide. From these strips, cut 2 **short rectangles** $2\frac{1}{2}$" x $8\frac{1}{2}$", 6 **medium rectangles** $2\frac{1}{2}$" x $10\frac{1}{2}$", and 4 **long rectangles** $2\frac{1}{2}$" x $12\frac{1}{2}$".**

From fabric for binding:

- Cut 8 **binding strips** $2\frac{1}{4}$" wide.

* You will need a **total** of 16 **triangles** for Side Blocks. The model was made using 2 triangles from each of 5 different fabrics and 1 triangle from each of 6 different fabrics.

** You will use a total of 64 medium rectangles and 40 long rectangles and will have 8 extra of each size.

Making The Blocks And Side Blocks

*Follow **Piecing** and **Pressing**, page 40. Match right sides and use a $\frac{1}{4}$" seam allowance.*

1. For each Block you will need, 1 **short rectangle**, 2 **medium rectangles**, and 1 **long rectangle** from one fabric and 1 **square** from a contrasting fabric.
2. Sew **short rectangle** to right edge of **square** to make **Unit 1**.
3. Turn Unit 1 one quarter turn to the left. Sew 1 **medium rectangle** to the right edge to make **Unit 2**.
4. Turn Unit 2 one quarter turn to the left. Sew 1 **medium rectangle** to the right edge to make **Unit 3**.
5. Turn Unit 3 one quarter turn to the left. Sew **long rectangle** to the right edge to make **Block**. Make 24 Blocks.

Unit 1

Unit 2

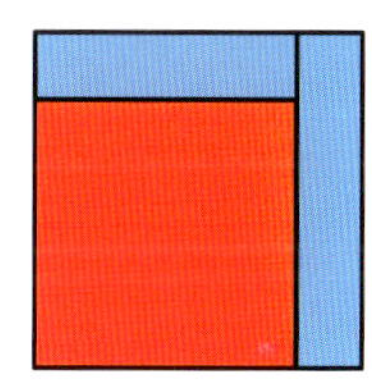

Unit 3

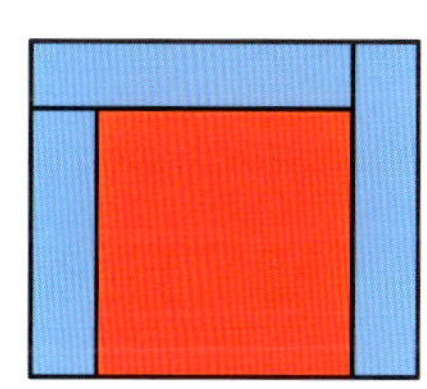

Block (make 24)

6. For each Side Block you will need, 1 **medium rectangle** and 1 **long rectangle** from one fabric and 1 **triangle** from a contrasting fabric.

7. Sew **medium rectangle** to 1 short edge of **triangle** to make **Unit 4**.

8. Sew **long rectangle** to remaining short edge of triangle. Trim rectangles even with long edge of triangle **(Fig. 1)** to make **Side Block**. Make 16 Side Blocks.

Unit 4

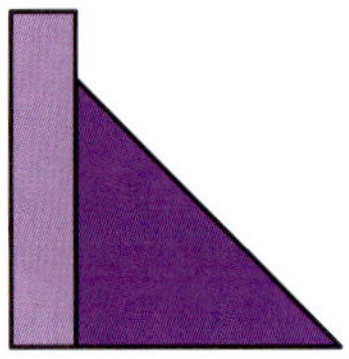

Fig. 1

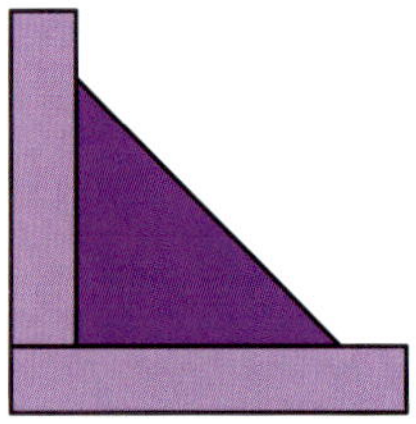

Side Block (make 16)

Assembling The Quilt Top

*Refer to **Assembly Diagram** to assemble the quilt top.*

1. Arrange Blocks and Side Blocks into 8 diagonal rows. Label rows 1-8.

2. Keeping block placement the same as your arrangement, sew Blocks and Side Blocks together into **Rows**.

3. Sew Rows together to make **Quilt Top**.

Completing The Quilt

1. Follow **Quilting**, page 41, to mark, layer, and quilt as desired. The model is machine quilted with an all-over flower and leaf pattern.

2. If desired, follow **Adding A Hanging Sleeve**, page 43, to add a hanging sleeve.

3. Use **binding strips** and follow **Binding**, page 44, to make and attach **straight-grain binding**. ◆

Assembly Diagram

gypsy Caravan

Finished Quilt Size: 49½" x 61½" (126 cm x 156 cm)
Finished Block Size: 9" x 9" (23 cm x 23 cm)

Fabric Requirements

Yardage is based on 43"/44" (109 cm/112 cm) wide fabric with a usable width of 40" (102 cm). Fat quarters are approximately 21" x 18" (53 cm x 46 cm). A layer cake square is 10" x 10" (25 cm x 25 cm).

- 13 assorted print fat quarters *or* 13 layer cake squares
- ⅛ yd (11 cm) ***each*** of 6 assorted small print or solid color fabrics
- ½ yd (46 cm) of yellow print fabric
- ¼ yd (23 cm) of brown solid color fabric
- 1⅞ yds (1.7 m) of stripe fabric
- 3⅞ yds (3.5 m) of fabric for backing

You will also need:

- 57" x 69" (145 cm x 175 cm) piece of batting

Cutting

Follow ***Rotary Cutting****, page 39, to cut fabric. Cut all strips from the selvage-to-selvage width of the fabric. All measurements include $^1/_4$" seam allowances.*

From **each** fat quarter or layer cake square:

- Cut 1 **center square** $9^1/_2$" x $9^1/_2$".

From assorted small print or solid color fabrics:

- Cut a ***total*** of 52 **squares** $3^1/_2$" x $3^1/_2$".

From yellow print fabric:

- Cut 2 strips $3^1/_2$" wide. From these strips, cut 8 **small rectangles** $3^1/_2$" x $9^1/_2$".
- Cut 1 strip $6^1/_2$" wide. From this strip, cut 4 **large rectangles** $6^1/_2$" x $9^1/_2$".

From brown solid color fabric:

- Cut 2 **top/bottom inner borders** $1^1/_4$" x 35".
- Cut 2 **side inner borders** $1^1/_4$" x $45^1/_2$", piecing as necessary.

From stripe fabric:

- Cut 2 **top/bottom outer borders** $7^1/_2$" x 49", piecing as necessary.
- Cut 2 **side outer borders** $7^1/_2$" x 47", piecing as necessary.
- Cut 1 **binding square** 23" x 23".

Making The Blocks

Follow ***Piecing*** *and* ***Pressing****, page 40. Match right sides and use a $^1/_4$" seam allowance.* ***Note:*** *The corner triangles (made from the squares) of adjacent blocks form diamonds because like fabrics are touching. To achieve this look, arrange all your block centers on a design wall or large flat surface and audition the placement of the squares before sewing them to the block centers.*

1. Place 1 assorted **square** on each corner of 1 **center square**. Stitch diagonally across small squares; trim $^1/_4$" from stitching lines (**Fig. 1**).

2. Press open to make **Snowball Block**. Make 13 Snowball Blocks.

Fig. 1

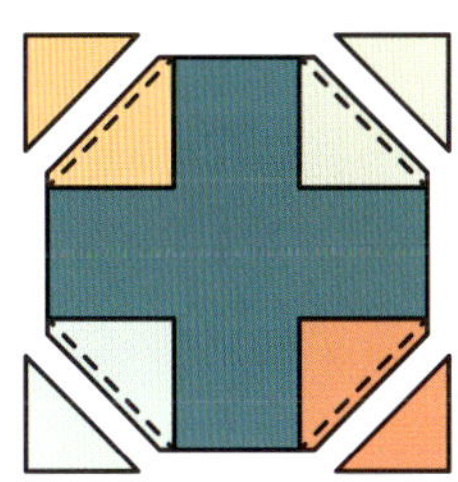

Snowball Block (make 13)

Assembling The Quilt Top

*Refer to **Quilt Top Diagram** to assemble the quilt top.*

1. Keeping block placement the same as your design wall, sew 3 Snowball Blocks and 2 **small rectangles** together to make **Row 1**. Make 3 Row 1's.

2. Sew 2 Snowball Blocks, 2 **large rectangles**, and 1 **small rectangle** together to make **Row 2**. Make 2 Row 2's.

3. Alternating Rows 1 and 2, sew Rows together to make **Quilt Top Center**.

4. Matching centers and corners, sew **side** then **top/bottom inner borders** to Quilt Top Center.

5. Matching centers and corners, sew **side** then **top/bottom outer borders** to Quilt Top Center to complete the **Quilt Top**.

Row 1 (make 3)

Row 2 (make 2)

Completing The Quilt

1. Follow **Quilting**, page 41, to mark, layer, and quilt as desired. The model is machine quilted with an all-over flower and leaf pattern.
2. If desired, follow **Adding A Hanging Sleeve**, page 43, to add a hanging sleeve.
3. Use **binding square** and follow **Binding**, page 44, to make and attach **bias binding**. ◆

Quilt Top Diagram

jeweled skylights

Finished Quilt Size: 51" x 69" (130 cm x 175 cm)
Finished Block Size: 9" x 9" (23 cm x 23 cm)

Fabric Requirements

Yardage is based on 43"/44" (109 cm/112 cm) wide fabric with a usable width of 40" (102 cm). A fat quarter is approximately 18" x 22" (46 cm x 56 cm).

27 fat quarters of batik fabrics: 3 golds, 3 light purples, 3 purples, 3 light greens, 3 greens, 3 blues, 3 oranges, 3 pinks, and 3 plums
1/4 yd (23 cm) of lavender solid color fabric
1 3/4 yds (1.6 m) of purple batik fabric
4 3/8 yds (4 m) of fabric for backing

You will also need:

59" x 77" (150 cm x 196 cm) piece of batting

Cutting

*Follow **Rotary Cutting**, page 39, to cut fabric. Cut all strips from the selvage-to-selvage width of the fabric. All measurements include ¼" seam allowances.*

From 1 gold batik fat quarter:
- Cut 5 **block centers** 6½" x 6½".

From *each* remaining gold batik fat quarter:
- Cut 5 **small squares** 2" x 2".
- Cut 5 **squares** 2⅝" x 2⅝".
- Cut 10 **block borders** 2" x 6½".

From 1 purple, 1 green, and 1 orange batik fat quarter:
- Cut 3 **block centers** 6½" x 6½" (9 total).

From *each* remaining purple, green, and orange batik fat quarter:
- Cut 3 **small squares** 2" x 2".
- Cut 3 **squares** 2⅝" x 2⅝".
- Cut 6 **block borders** 2" x 6½".

From 1 light purple, 1 light green, 1 blue, 1 pink, and 1 plum batik fat quarter:
- Cut 2 **block centers** 6½" x 6½" (10 total)

From *each* remaining light purple, light green, blue, pink, and plum fat quarter:
- Cut 2 **small squares** 2" x 2".
- Cut 2 **squares** 2⅝" x 2⅝".
- Cut 4 **block borders** 2" x 6½".

From lavender solid color fabric:
- Cut 2 **side inner borders** 1½" x 54½", piecing as necessary.
- Cut 2 **top/bottom inner borders** 1½" x 38½".

From purple batik fabric:
- Cut 2 **side outer borders** 6½" x 56½", piecing as necessary.
- Cut 2 **top/bottom borders** 6½" x 50½", piecing as necessary.
- Cut 7 **binding strips** 2¼" wide.

Making The Blocks

*Follow **Piecing** and **Pressing**, page 40. Match right sides and use a ¼" seam allowance. Refer to **Block Diagram**, page 18, for fabric placement.*

1. For each Block, from *one color group* of batik fabrics you will need 1 **block center** from 1 fabric and 1 **small square**, 1 **square**, and 2 **block borders** from *each* of the two coordinating fabrics.

2. Draw a diagonal line on wrong side of 1 **square**.

3. Matching right sides, place 1 marked square on top of 1 unmarked square. Stitch ¼" from each side of drawn line (**Fig. 1**). Cut along drawn line and press seam allowances toward darker fabric to make 2 **Triangle-Squares**. Trim Triangle-Squares to 2" x 2".

Fig. 1

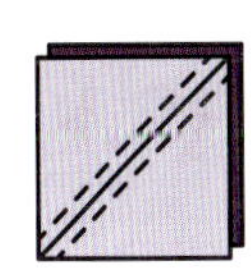

Triangle-Square (make 2)

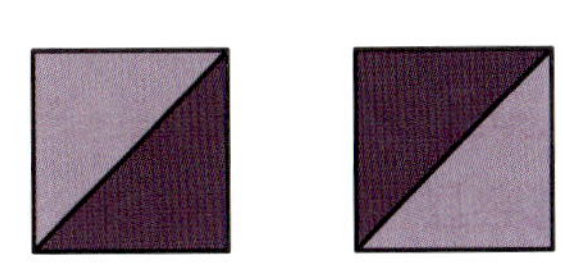

4. Sew 1 **block border** to either side of **block center** to make **Unit 1**.

5. Sew 1 **small square** and 1 Triangle-Square to either end of 1 block border to make **Unit 2.** Make 2 Unit 2's.

6. Sew 1 Unit 2 to top and bottom edges of Unit 1 to complete **Block**. Make 24 Blocks.

Unit 1

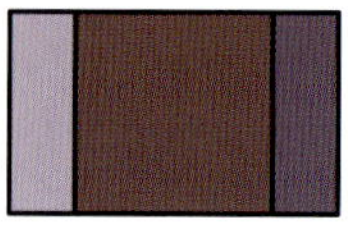

Unit 2 (make 2)

Assembling The Quilt Top

Refer to ***Quilt Top Diagram*** *for Block orientation when assembling the quilt top.*

1. Sew 4 Blocks together to make **Row**. Make 6 Rows.

2. Sew Rows together to make **Quilt Top Center**.

3. Matching centers and corners, sew **side** then **top/bottom inner borders** to Quilt Top Center.

4. Matching centers and corners, sew **side** then **top/bottom outer borders** to Quilt Top Center to complete **Quilt Top**.

Block (make 24)

Row (make 6)

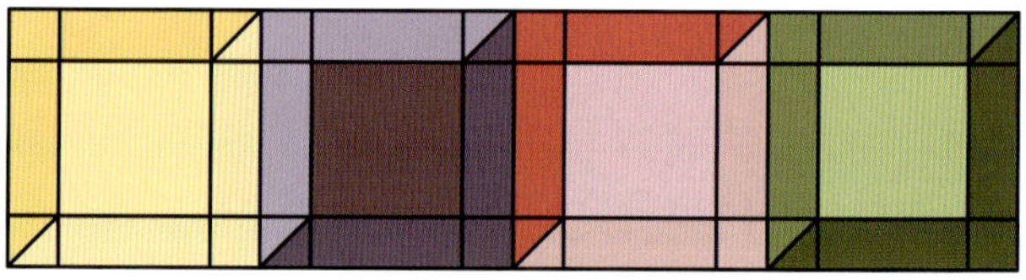

Completing The Quilt

1. Follow **Quilting**, page 41, to mark, layer, and quilt as desired. The model is machine quilted with all-over meander quilting.

2. If desired, follow **Adding A Hanging Sleeve**, page 43, to add a hanging sleeve.

3. Use **binding strips** and follow **Binding**, page 44, to make and attach **straight-grain binding**. ◆

Quilt Top Diagram

josie's quilt

Finished Quilt Size: 49" x 67" (124 cm x 170 cm)
Finished Block Size: 6" x 9" (15 cm x 23 cm)

Fabric Requirements

Yardage is based on 43"/44" (109 cm/112 cm) wide fabric with a usable width of 40" (102 cm). Fat quarters are approximately 21" x 18" (53 cm x 46 cm).

- 6 assorted print fat quarters
- $\frac{5}{8}$ yd (57 cm) of green dot fabric
- $\frac{1}{4}$ yd (23 cm) of purple dot fabric
- $\frac{5}{8}$ yd (57 cm) of uneven stripe fabric
- $1\frac{3}{4}$ yds (1.6 m) of wide stripe fabric
- $4\frac{1}{4}$ yds (3.9 m) of fabric for backing

You will also need:

- 57" x 75" (145 cm x 191 cm) piece of batting

Cutting

*Follow **Rotary Cutting**, page 39, to cut fabric. Cut all strips from the selvage-to-selvage width of the fabric. All measurements include $\frac{1}{4}$" seam allowances.*

From **each** fat quarter:

- Cut 3 **rectangles** $6\frac{1}{2}$" x $9\frac{1}{2}$".

From green dot fabric:

- Cut 5 **strips** $3\frac{1}{2}$" wide.

From purple dot fabric:

- Cut 2 **top/bottom inner borders** $1\frac{1}{2}$" x $36\frac{1}{2}$".
- Cut 2 **side inner borders** $1\frac{1}{2}$" x $56\frac{1}{2}$", piecing as necessary.

From uneven stripe fabric:

- Cut 5 **strips** $3\frac{1}{2}$" wide.

From wide stripe fabric:

- Cut 2 **top/bottom outer borders** $5\frac{1}{2}$" x $38\frac{1}{2}$".
- Cut 2 **side outer borders** $5\frac{1}{2}$" x $66\frac{1}{2}$", piecing as necessary.
- Cut 1 **binding square** 24" x 24".

Making The Blocks

*Follow **Piecing** and **Pressing**, page 40. Match right sides and use a $\frac{1}{4}$" seam allowance.*

1. Matching long edges, sew 1 green dot **strip** and 1 uneven stripe **strip** together to make **Strip Set**. Make 5 Strip Sets. Cut across Strip Sets at 5" intervals to make **Unit 1**. Make 36 Unit 1's.

2. Referring to **Block A Diagram**, sew 2 Unit 1's together to make **Block A**. Make 9 Block A's.

3. Referring to **Block B Diagram**, sew 2 Unit 1's together to make **Block B**. Make 9 Block B's.

Strip Set
(make 5)

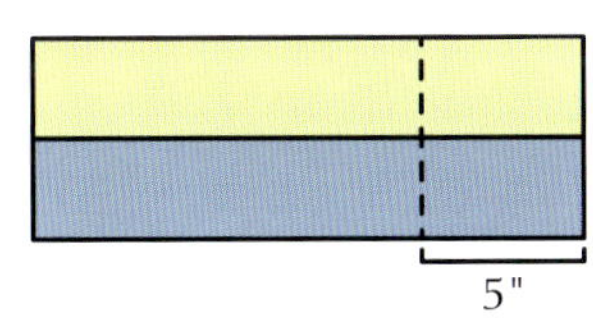

Unit 1
(make 36)

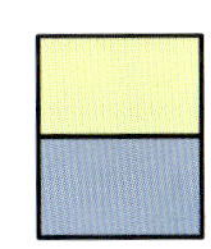

Block A
(make 9)

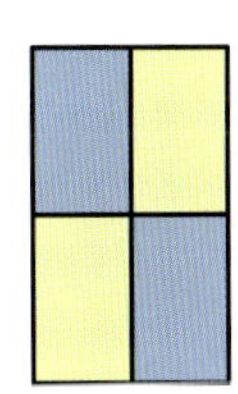

Block B
(make 9)

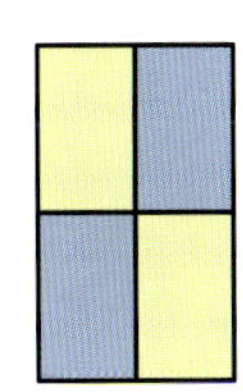

Assembling The Quilt Top

*Refer to **Quilt Top Diagram** to assemble the quilt top.*

1. Sew 3 Block A's and 3 **rectangles** together to make **Row 1**. Make 3 Row 1's.

2. Sew 3 Block B's and 3 **rectangles** together to make **Row 2**. Make 3 Row 2's.

3. Alternating Rows 1 and 2, sew Rows together to make **Quilt Top Center**.

4. Matching centers and corners, sew **top/bottom** then **side inner borders** to Quilt Top Center.

5. Matching centers and corners, sew **top/bottom** then **side outer borders** to Quilt Top Center to complete the **Quilt Top**.

Row 1 (make 3)

Row 2 (make 3)

Completing The Quilt

1. Follow **Quilting**, page 41, to mark, layer, and quilt as desired. The model is machine quilted with an all-over flower and leaf pattern.
2. If desired, follow **Adding A Hanging Sleeve**, page 43, to add a hanging sleeve.
3. Use **binding square** and follow **Binding**, page 44, to make and attach **bias binding**.

Quilt Top Diagram

josie's quilt

Finished Quilt Size: 37" x 49" (94 cm x 124 cm)
Finished Block Size: 6" x 9" (15 cm x 23 cm)

Fabric Requirements

Yardage is based on 43"/44" (109 cm/112 cm) wide fabric with a usable width of 40" (102 cm). Fat quarters are approximately 21" x 18" (53 cm x 46 cm).

- 4 assorted print fat quarters
- 8 assorted 8" x 6" (20 cm x 15 cm) small print rectangles: 1 brown, 1 pink/brown, **2** pinks, 2 greens, and 2 aquas
- 1/4 yd (23 cm) of white solid fabric
- 3/4 yd (69 m) of green print fabric
- 1/4 yd (23 cm) of pink solid fabric
- 3/8 yd (34 cm) of pink dot fabric
- 3 1/4 yds (3 m) of fabric for backing

You will also need:

- 45" x 57" (114 cm x 145 cm) piece of batting

Cutting

*Follow **Rotary Cutting**, page 39, to cut fabric. Cut all strips from the selvage-to-selvage width of the fabric. All measurements include $^{1}/_{4}$" seam allowances.*

From **each** fat quarter:

- Cut 2 **large rectangles** $6^{1}/_{2}$" x $9^{1}/_{2}$".

From **each** small print rectangle:

- Cut 2 **small rectangles** $3^{1}/_{2}$" x 5".

From white solid fabric:

- Cut 2 strips $3^{1}/_{2}$" wide. From these strips, cut 16 **small rectangles** $3^{1}/_{2}$" x 5".

From green print fabric:

- Cut 2 **top/bottom outer borders** $5^{1}/_{2}$" x $36^{1}/_{2}$".
- Cut 2 **side outer borders** $5^{1}/_{2}$" x $38^{1}/_{2}$".

From pink solid fabric:

- Cut 2 **top/bottom inner borders** $1^{1}/_{2}$" x $26^{1}/_{2}$".
- Cut 2 **side inner borders** $1^{1}/_{2}$" x $36^{1}/_{2}$".

From pink dot fabric:

- Cut 5 **binding strips** $2^{1}/_{4}$" wide.

Making The Blocks

*Follow **Piecing** and **Pressing**, page 40. Match right sides and use a $^{1}/_{4}$" seam allowance.*

1. Sew 2 white **small rectangles**, 1 brown **small rectangle** and 1 pink/brown **small rectangle** together to make **Block A**. Make 2 Block A's.

2. Repeat Step 1 using 2 white **small rectangles** and 2 assorted pink **small rectangles** to make **Block B**. Make 2 Block B's.

3. Repeat Step 1 using 2 white **small rectangles** and 2 assorted aqua **small rectangles** to make **Block C**. Make 2 Block C's.

4. Repeat Step 1 using 2 white **small rectangles** and 2 assorted green **small rectangles** to make **Block D**. Make 2 Block D's.

Block A
(make 2)

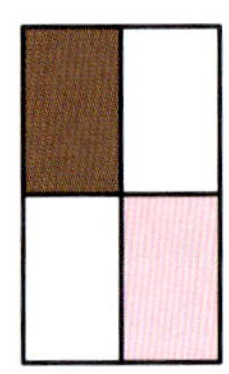

Block B
(make 2)

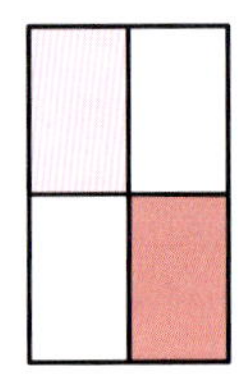

Block C
(make 2)

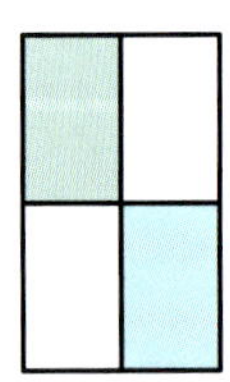

Block D
(make 2)

Assembling The Quilt Top

*Refer to **Quilt Top Diagram** to assemble the quilt top.*

1. Sew 2 **large rectangles,** 1 Block A, and 1 Block B together to make **Row 1**. Make 2 Row 1's.

2. Sew 2 **large rectangles,** 1 Block C, and 1 Block D together to make **Row 2**. Make 2 Row 2's.

3. Alternating Rows 1 and 2, sew Rows together to make **Quilt Top Center**.

4. Matching centers and corners, sew **side** then **top/bottom inner borders** to Quilt Top Center.

5. Matching centers and corners, sew **side** then **top/bottom outer borders** to Quilt Top Center to complete **Quilt Top**.

Row 1 (make 2)

Row 2 (make 2)

Quilt Top Diagram

Completing The Quilt

1. Follow **Quilting**, page 41, to mark, layer, and quilt as desired. The model is machine quilted with an all-over leaf and swirl pattern.

2. If desired, follow **Adding A Hanging Sleeve**, page 43, to add a hanging sleeve.

3. Use **binding strips** and follow **Binding**, page 44, to make and attach **straight-grain binding**. ◆

madison avenue

1

Finished Quilt Size: 51" x 70" (130 cm x 178 cm)
Finished Block Size: 20" x 20" (51 cm x 51 cm)

Fabric Requirements

Yardage is based on 43"/44" (109 cm/112 cm) wide fabric with a usable width of 40" (102 cm). A fat quarter is approximately 18" x 22" (46 cm x 56 cm).

- 20 fat quarters of assorted print fabrics: 5 yellows, 5 greens, 5 blues, and 5 reds
- 1 1/4 yds (1.1 m) of white solid fabric
- 1/2 yd (46 cm) of white print fabric
- 3/4 yd (69 cm) of grey polka dot fabric
- 5" x 10" (13 cm x 25 cm) rectangle of yellow wool
- 4" x 8" (10 cm x 20 cm) rectangle of red wool
- 1/2 yd (46 cm) of fabric for binding
- 4 3/8 yds (4 m) of fabric for backing

You will also need:

- 2 1/2 yds (2.3 m) of green jumbo rick rack
- Yellow and red #5 pearl cotton
- Two 5/8" (16 mm) dia. buttons
- 59" x 78" (150 cm x 198 cm) piece of batting

Cutting

*Follow **Rotary Cutting**, page 39, to cut fabric. All measurements include $^1/_4$" seam allowances. Flower patterns are found on page 36.*

From **each color group** of 5 assorted fat quarters:

- Cut 1 **center square** 3" x 3".
- Cut 1 **rectangle** $2^1/_2$" x 3" (**A**).
- Cut 2 **rectangles** $2^1/_2$" x 5" (**B** and **C**).
- Cut 2 **rectangles** $2^1/_2$" x 7" (**D** and **E**).
- Cut 2 **rectangles** $2^1/_2$" x 9" (**F** and **G**).
- Cut 2 **rectangles** $2^1/_2$" x 11" (**H** and **I**).
- Cut 2 **rectangles** $2^1/_2$" x 13" (**J** and **K**).
- Cut 1 **rectangle** $2^1/_2$" x 15" (**L**).
- Cut 8 **border rectangles** 3" x $10^1/_2$".*

*You will use 32 border rectangles and discard 8.

From white solid color fabric:

- Cut 8 squares 13" x 13". Cut each square in half *once* diagonally to make 16 **triangles**.

From white print fabric:

- Cut 2 **top/bottom borders** 5" x $40^1/_2$", piecing as necessary.
- Cut 2 **side border accents** $1^1/_2$" x $5^1/_2$".

From grey polka dot fabric:

- Cut 4 **side border strips** $5^1/_2$" x $34^1/_2$".

From yellow wool:

- Cut 2 **large flowers**.

From red wool:

- Cut 2 **small flowers**.

From fabric for binding:

- Cut 7 **binding strips** $2^1/_4$" wide.

Making The Blocks

*Follow **Piecing** and **Pressing**, page 40. Match right sides and use a $^1/_4$" seam allowance.*

1. For each Block from *one color group* you will need, 1 **center square** and 1 of each **rectangle A-L**.

2. Sew **rectangle A** to right edge of **center square** (**Fig. 1**).

3. Turn center square $^1/_4$ turn to the left. Sew **rectangle B** to the right edge (**Fig. 2**).

4. Turn center square $^1/_4$ turn to the left. Sew **rectangle C** to the right edge (**Fig. 3**).

Fig. 1

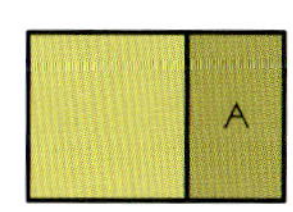

Fig. 2

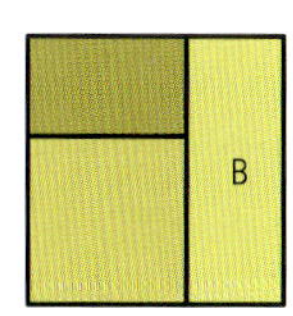

Fig. 3

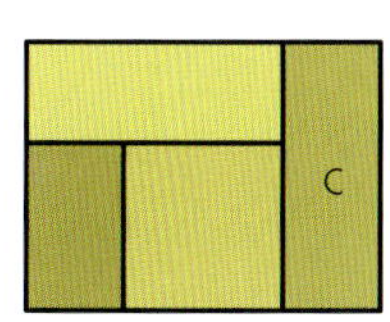

5. In the same manner, continue adding **rectangles D-L** to make **Block Center**. Trim Block Center to 12$^1/_2$" x 12$^1/_2$".

6. Repeat Steps 1-5 using center squares and rectangles A-L from remaining 3 color groups to make 4 Block Centers.

7. Sew 1 **triangle** to opposite sides of a Block Center. Trim points of triangles even with edges of Block Center (**Fig. 4**). **Note:** Triangles are overcut to allow Block Centers to "float" on white backgrounds.

8. Sew 1 triangle to each remaining side to make **Block**. Centering Block Center, trim Block to 20$^1/_2$" x 20$^1/_2$". Make 4 Blocks.

Block Center (make 4)

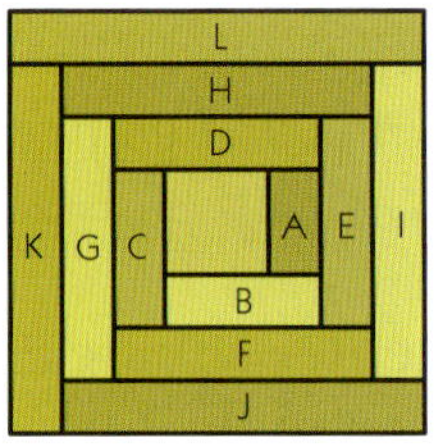

Fig. 4

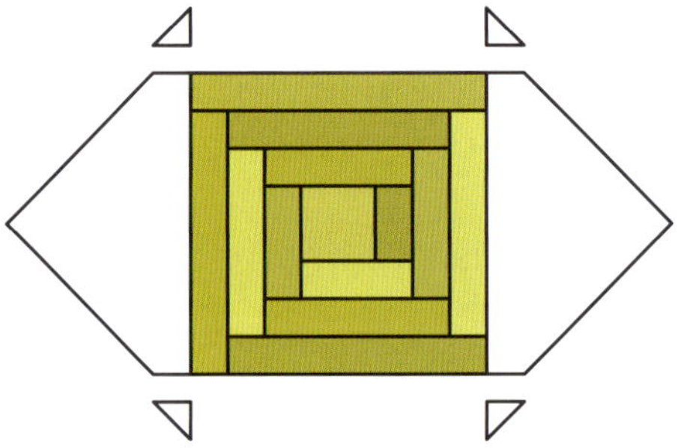

Assembling The Quilt Top

*Refer to **Quilt Top Diagram** to assemble the quilt top.*

1. Sew 2 Blocks together to make **Row**. Make 2 Rows.

2. Sew Rows together to make **Quilt Top Center**.

3. Arranging colors and fabrics as desired, match long edges and sew 16 **border rectangles** together to make **Inner Border**. Make 2 Inner Borders.

4. Matching centers and corners, sew **Inner Borders** to opposite sides of Quilt Top Center.

5. Matching centers and corners, sew **top/bottom borders** to the Quilt Top Center.

6. Cut **rickrack** in half. Center and sew 1 length of rickrack to each top/bottom border; trim excess even with sides of Quilt Top.

Block (make 4)

Inner Border (make 2)

7. Sew 1 **side border accent** and 2 **side border strips** together to make **Side Border**. Make 2 Side Borders.

8. Matching centers and corners, sew Side Borders to Quilt Top Center.

9. Use pearl cotton to **Blanket Stitch (Fig. 5)** 1 **large** and 1 **small flower** to each top and bottom border to complete the **Quilt Top**.

Side Border (make 2)

Fig. 5

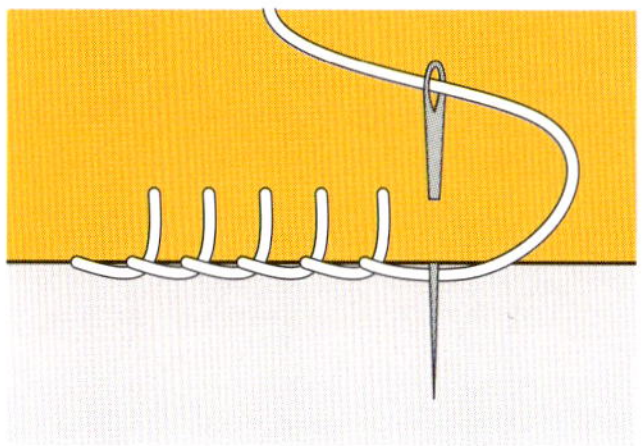

Completing The Quilt

1. Follow **Quilting**, page 41, to mark, layer, and quilt as desired. The model is machine quilted with an all-over loop and swirl pattern.

2. If desired, follow **Adding A Hanging Sleeve**, page 43, to add a hanging sleeve.

3. Use **binding strips** and follow **Binding**, page 44, to make and attach **straight-grain binding**.

4. Stitching through all layers, sew one button in the center of each flower.◆

Quilt Top Diagram

madison avenue 2

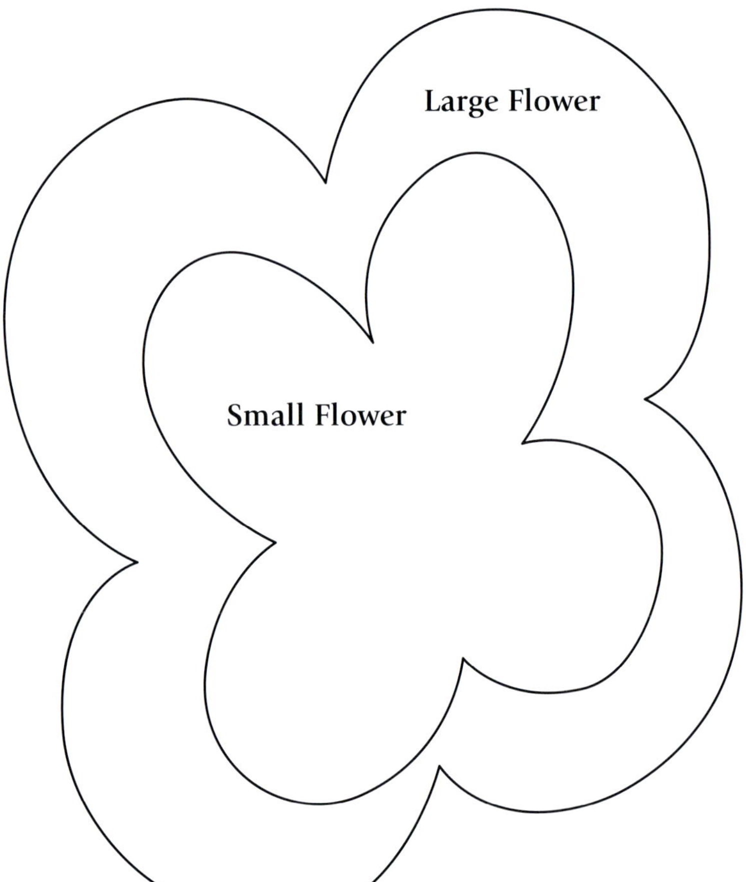

If retro fabrics are more your style, grab some reproduction prints and follow the instructions for Madison Avenue 1, page 30, with the following exceptions:

- Side borders do not have accent strips. Cut 2 side borders $5\frac{1}{2}$" x $69\frac{1}{2}$", piecing as necessary.
- Instead of adding rickrack to the top and bottom borders, make pieced borders by sewing 1 white solid 3" x $40\frac{1}{2}$" strip, 1 print $1\frac{1}{2}$" x $40\frac{1}{2}$" strip, and 1 white solid $1\frac{1}{2}$" x $40\frac{1}{2}$" strip together for each border.
- Follow **Fusible Appliqué**, page 41, to cut 2 large and 2 small flowers from fabric scraps.
- Stitch around the flower edges using your preferred method of appliqué. **Note:** Flowers on the model were machine Blanket Stitched. ♦

general instructions

To make your quilting easier and more enjoyable, we encourage you to carefully read all of the general instructions, study the color photographs, and familiarize yourself with the individual project instructions before beginning a project.

Fabrics

SELECTING FABRICS

Choose high-quality, medium-weight 100% cotton fabrics. All-cotton fabrics hold a crease better, fray less, and are easier to quilt than cotton/polyester blends.

Yardage requirements listed for each project are based on 43"/44" wide fabric with a "usable" width of 40" after shrinkage and trimming selvages. Actual usable width will probably vary slightly from fabric to fabric. Our recommended yardage lengths should be adequate for occasional re-squaring of fabric when many cuts are required.

PREPARING FABRICS

Pre-washing fabrics may cause edges to ravel. As a result, your fat quarters or other pre-cut fabric pieces may not be large enough to cut all of the pieces required for your chosen project. Therefore, we do not recommend pre-washing your yardage or pre-cut fabrics. Refer to **Caring For Your Quilt**, page 48, for instructions on washing your finished quilt. Before cutting, prepare fabrics with a steam iron set on cotton and starch or sizing. The starch or sizing will give the fabric a crisp finish. This will make cutting more accurate and may make piecing easier.

Rotary Cutting

CUTTING FROM YARDAGE

- Place fabric on work surface with fold closest to you.
- Cut all strips from the selvage-to-selvage width of the fabric.
- Square left edge of fabric using rotary cutter and rulers (**Figs. 1-2**).
- To cut each strip required for a project, place ruler over cut edge of fabric, aligning desired marking on ruler with cut edge; make cut (**Fig. 3**).
- When cutting several strips from a single piece of fabric, it is important to make sure that cuts remain at a perfect right angle to the fold; square fabric as needed.

CUTTING FROM FAT QUARTERS

- Place fabric flat on work surface with lengthwise (18") edge closest to you.
- Square long (21") left edge of fabric in the same manner as above.
- Cut all strips parallel to the 21" edge of fabric.
- To cut each strip required for a project, place ruler over cut edge of fabric, aligning desired marking on ruler with cut edge; make cut.

Fig. 1

Fig. 2

Fig. 3

Piecing

Precise cutting, followed by accurate piecing, will ensure that all pieces of the quilt top fit together well.

- Set sewing machine stitch length for approximately 11 stitches per inch.
- Use neutral-colored general-purpose sewing thread (not quilting thread) in needle and in bobbin.
- An accurate $^1/_4$" seam allowance is essential. Presser feet that are $^1/_4$" wide are available for most sewing machines.
- When piecing, always place pieces right sides together and match raw edges; pin if necessary.
- Chain piecing saves time and will usually result in more accurate piecing.
- Trim away points of seam allowances that extend beyond the edges of the sewn pieces.

Sewing Across Seam Intersections

When sewing across intersection of two seams, place pieces right sides together and match seams exactly, making sure seam allowances are pressed in opposite directions (**Fig. 4**).

Fig. 4

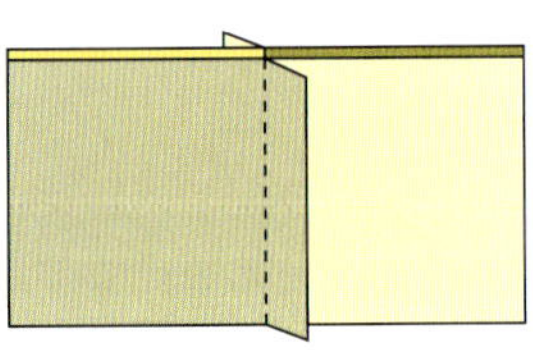

Sewing Sharp Points

To ensure sharp points when joining triangular or diagonal pieces, stitch across the center of the "X" (shown in pink) formed on wrong side by previous seams (**Fig. 5**).

Fig. 5

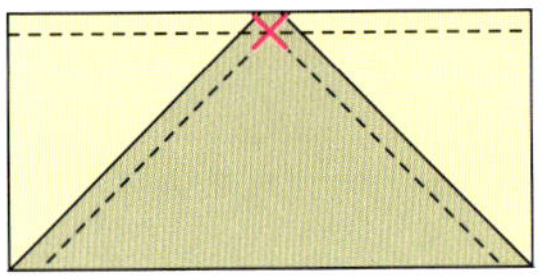

Pressing

- Use steam iron set on "Cotton" for all pressing.
- Press after sewing each seam.
- Seam allowances are almost always pressed to one side, usually toward the darker fabric. However, to reduce bulk it may occasionally be necessary to press seam allowances toward the lighter fabric or even to press them open.
- To prevent a dark fabric seam allowance from showing through light fabric, trim the darker seam allowance slightly narrower than the lighter seam allowance.
- To press long seams, such as those in long strip sets, without curving or other distortion, lay strips across the width of the ironing board.

Fusible Appliqué

White or light-colored fabrics may need to be lined with fusible interfacing before applying fusible web to prevent darker fabrics from showing through.

1. Place paper-backed fusible web, paper side up, over appliqué pattern. Trace pattern onto paper side of web with a pencil as many times as indicated in project instructions for a single fabric.
2. Follow manufacturer's instructions to fuse traced patterns to wrong side of fabrics. Do not remove paper backing.
3. Use scissors to cut out appliqué pieces along traced lines. Remove paper backing from all pieces. Follow manufacturer's instructions to fuse appliqué pieces in place.

Quilting

Quilting holds the three layers (top, batting, and backing) of the quilt together and can be done by hand or machine. Because marking, layering, and quilting are interrelated and may be done in different orders depending on circumstances, please read entire Quilting section, pages 41–43, before beginning project.

TYPES OF QUILTING DESIGNS

All-Over Quilting

Quilting with a continuous design is called "all-over" quilting. Possible designs include leaves, vines, flowers, loops, swirls, or even a combination of two or more designs. This type of quilting can be free-form or it can be marked.

Meandering Quilting

Quilting in random curved lines and swirls is called "meandering" quilting. Quilting lines should not cross or touch each other. This type of quilting does not need to be marked.

MARKING QUILTING LINES

Quilting lines may be marked using fabric marking pencils, chalk markers, water- or air-soluble pens, or lead pencils.

Simple quilting designs may be marked with chalk or chalk pencil after basting. A small area may be marked, then quilted, before moving to next area to be marked. Intricate designs should be marked before basting using a more durable marker.

Caution: Pressing may permanently set some marks. Test different markers on scrap fabric to find one that marks clearly and can be thoroughly removed.

A wide variety of pre-cut quilting stencils, as well as entire books of quilting patterns, are available. Using a stencil makes it easier to mark intricate or repetitive designs.

To make a stencil from a pattern, center template plastic over pattern and use a permanent marker to trace pattern onto plastic. Use a craft knife with single or double blade to cut channels along traced lines (**Fig. 6**).

Fig. 6

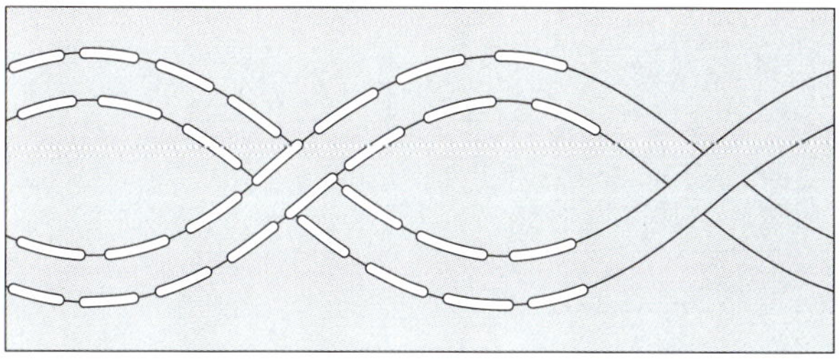

PREPARING THE BACKING

To allow for a slight shifting of the quilt top during quilting, the backing should be approximately 4" larger on all sides. Yardage requirements listed for quilt backings are calculated for 43"/44"w fabric. Using 90"w or 108"w fabric for the backing may eliminate piecing. To piece a backing using 43"/44"w fabric, use the following instructions.

1. Measure length and width of quilt top; add 8" to each measurement.
2. Cut backing fabric into two lengths slightly longer than determined length measurement. Trim selvages. Place lengths with right sides facing and sew long edges together, forming tube (**Fig. 7**). Match seams and press along one fold (**Fig. 8**). Cut along pressed fold to form single piece (**Fig. 9**).

Fig. 7 **Fig. 8** **Fig. 9**

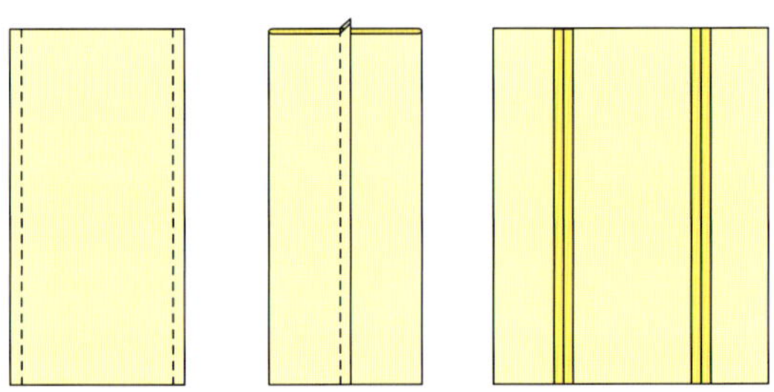

3. Trim backing to size determined in Step 1; press seam allowances open.

CHOOSING THE BATTING

The appropriate batting will make quilting easier. All cotton or cotton/polyester blend battings work well for machine quilting because the cotton helps "grip" quilt layers. If quilt is to be tied, a high-loft batting, sometimes called extra-loft or fat batting, may be used to make quilt "fluffy."

Types of batting include cotton, polyester, wool, cotton/polyester blend, cotton/wool blend, and silk.

When selecting batting, refer to package labels for characteristics and care instructions. Cut batting same size as prepared backing.

ASSEMBLING THE QUILT

1. Examine wrong side of quilt top closely; trim any seam allowances and clip any threads that may show through front of the quilt. Press quilt top, being careful not to "set" any marked quilting lines.
2. Place backing wrong side up on flat surface. Use masking tape to tape edges of backing to surface. Place batting on top of backing fabric. Smooth batting gently, being careful not to stretch or tear. Center quilt top right side up on batting.
3. Use 1" rustproof safety pins to "pin-baste" all layers together, spacing pins approximately 4" apart. Begin at the center and work toward the outer edges to secure all layers. If possible, place pins away from areas that will be quilted, although pins may be removed as needed when quilting.

MACHINE QUILTING METHODS

Use general-purpose thread in bobbin. Do not use quilting thread. Thread the needle with general-purpose thread or transparent monofilament thread to make quilting blend with quilt top fabrics. Use decorative thread, such as a metallic or contrasting-color general-purpose thread, to make quilting lines stand out more.

Straight-Line Quilting

The term "straight-line" is somewhat deceptive, since curves (especially gentle ones) as well as straight lines can be stitched with this technique.

1. Set stitch length for six to ten stitches per inch and attach a walking foot to the sewing machine.
2. Determine which section of the quilt will have the longest continuous quilting line, oftentimes the area from center top to center bottom. Roll up and secure each edge of the quilt to help reduce the bulk, keeping fabrics smooth. Smaller projects may not need to be rolled.
3. Begin stitching on longest quilting line, using very short stitches for the first $^{1}/_{4}$" to "lock" quilting. Stitch across project, using one hand on each side of walking foot to slightly spread fabric and to guide fabric through machine. Lock stitches at end of quilting line.
4. Continue machine quilting, stitching longer quilting lines first to stabilize quilt before moving on to other areas.

Free-Motion Quilting

Free-motion quilting may be free form or may follow a marked pattern.

1. Attach darning foot to sewing machine and lower or cover feed dogs.
2. Position quilt under darning foot; lower foot. Holding top thread, take a stitch and pull bobbin thread to top of quilt. To "lock" beginning of quilting line, hold top and bobbin threads while making three to five stitches in place.
3. Use one hand on each side of darning foot to slightly spread fabric and to move fabric through the machine. Even stitch length is achieved by using smooth, flowing hand motion and steady machine speed. Slow machine speed and fast hand movement will create long stitches. Fast machine speed and slow hand movement will create short stitches. Move quilt sideways, back and forth, in a circular motion, or in a random motion to create desired designs; do not rotate quilt. Lock stitches at end of each quilting line.

Adding A Hanging Sleeve

Attaching a hanging sleeve to back of wall hanging or quilt before the binding is added allows project to be displayed on wall.

1. Measure the width of quilt top edge and subtract 1". Cut a piece of fabric 7"w by determined measurement.
2. Press the short edges of fabric piece $^{1}/_{4}$" to the wrong side; press edges $^{1}/_{4}$" to the wrong side again and machine stitch in place.
3. Matching wrong sides, fold piece in half lengthwise to form a tube.
4. Follow project instructions to sew binding to the quilt top and to trim backing and batting. Before Blindstitching binding to backing, match raw edges and stitch hanging sleeve to the center top edge on the back of the quilt.
5. Finish binding quilt, treating hanging sleeve as part of backing.
6. Blindstitch bottom of hanging sleeve to backing, taking care not to stitch through to front of quilt.

Binding

Binding encloses the raw edges of quilt and may be cut from the bias or straight-grain of the fabric.

MAKING BIAS BINDING

When a long length of binding is needed, the "continuous" method, below, is quick and accurate.

1. Cut **binding square** in half diagonally to make two triangles.
2. With right sides together and using 1/4" seam allowance, sew triangles together (**Fig. 10**); press seam allowances open.

Fig. 10

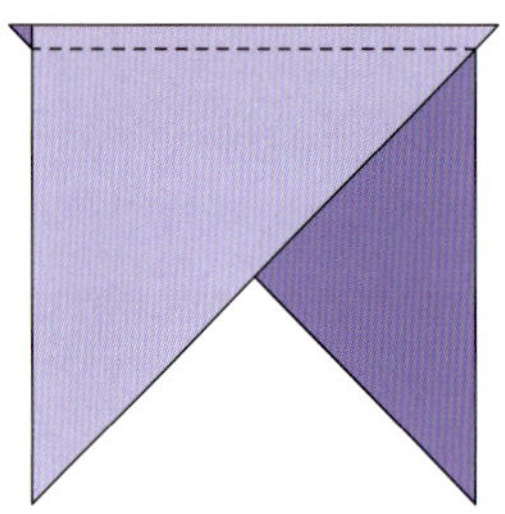

3. On wrong side of fabric, draw lines 2 1/4" apart (**Fig. 11**). Cut off any remaining fabric less than this width.

Fig. 11

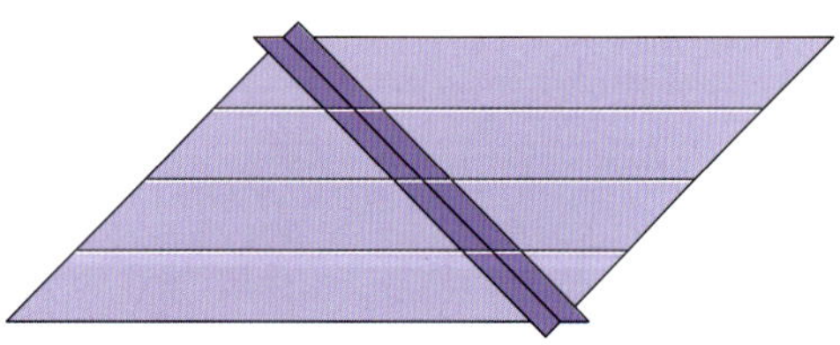

4. With right sides inside, bring short edges together to form tube; match raw edges so that first drawn line of top section meets second drawn line of bottom section (**Fig. 12**).

Fig. 12

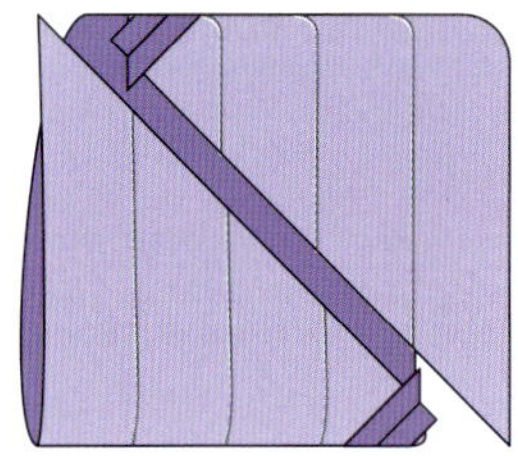

5. Carefully pin edges together by inserting pins through drawn lines at point where drawn lines intersect, making sure pins go through intersections on both sides. Using 1/4" seam allowance, sew edges together; press seam allowances open.
6. To cut a continuous strip, begin cutting along first drawn line (**Fig. 13**). Continue cutting along drawn line around tube.

Fig. 13

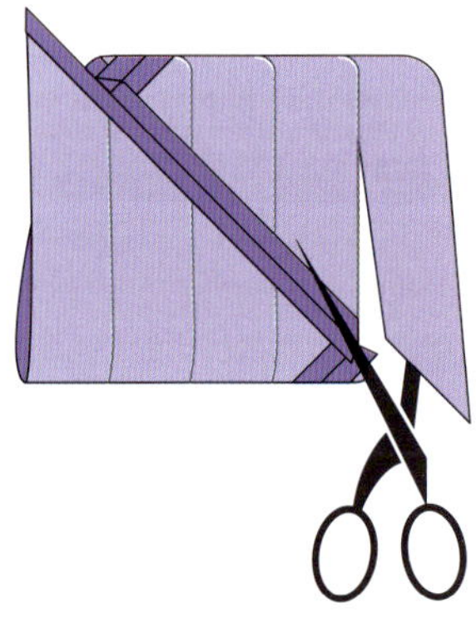

7. Trim ends of bias strip square.
8. Matching wrong sides and raw edges, carefully press bias strip in half lengthwise to complete binding.

MAKING STRAIGHT-GRAIN BINDING

1. To piece **binding strips**, use the diagonal seams method (**Fig. 14**).

Fig. 14

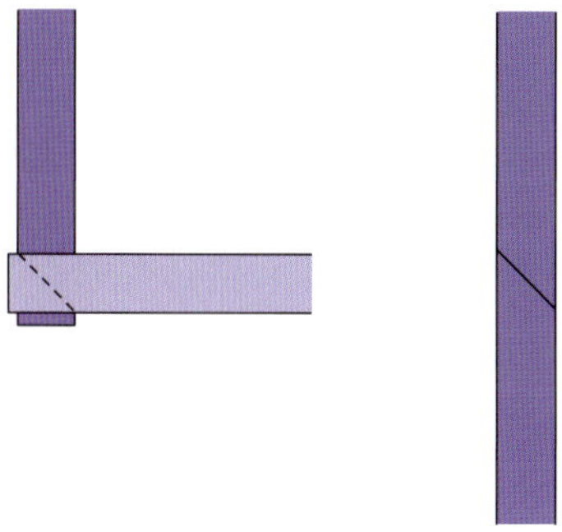

2. Matching wrong sides and raw edges, press strip(s) in half lengthwise to complete binding.

ATTACHING BINDING WITH MITERED CORNERS

1. Beginning with one end near center on bottom edge of quilt, lay binding around quilt to make sure that seams in binding will not end up at a corner. Adjust placement if necessary. Matching raw edges of binding to raw edge of quilt top, pin binding to right side of quilt along one edge.
2. When you reach first corner, mark 1/4" from corner of quilt top (**Fig. 15**).

Fig. 15

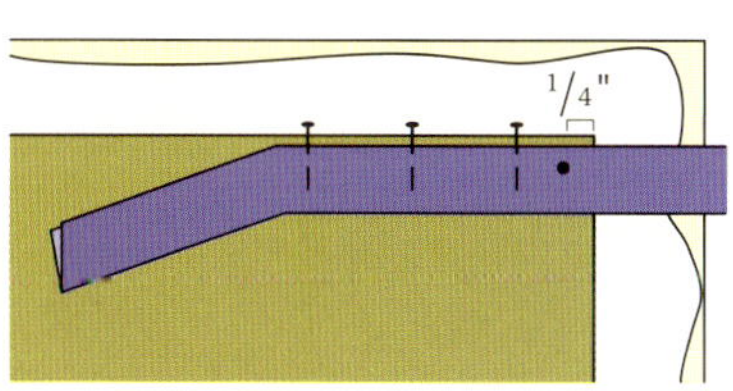

3. Beginning approximately 10" from end of binding and using a 1/4" seam allowance, sew binding to quilt, backstitching at beginning of stitching and at mark (**Fig. 16**). Lift needle out of fabric and clip thread.

Fig. 16

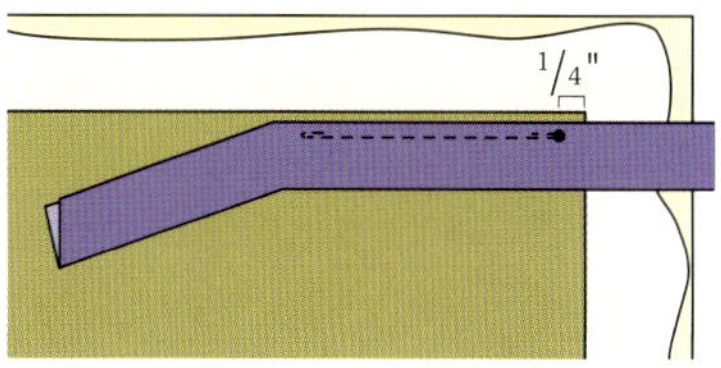

4. Fold binding as shown (**Figs. 17-18**) and pin binding to adjacent side, matching raw edges. When you've reached the next corner, mark 1/4" from edge of quilt top.

Fig. 17

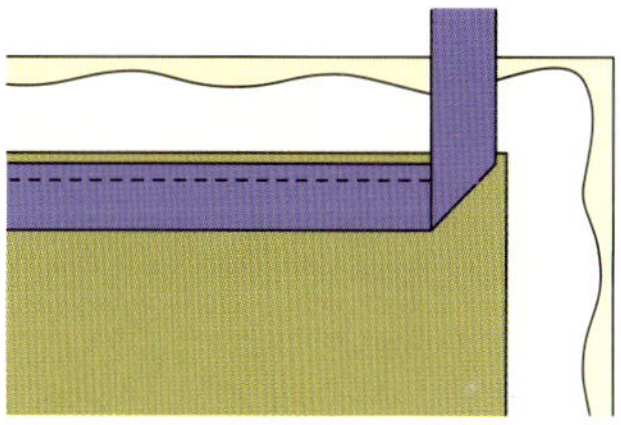

Fig. 18

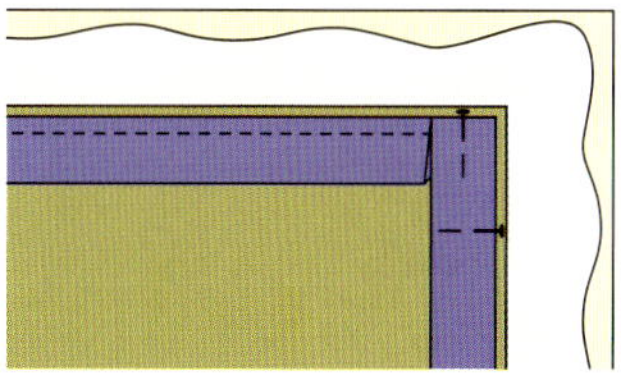

5. Backstitching at edge of quilt top, sew pinned binding to quilt (**Fig. 19**); backstitch at the next mark. Lift needle out of fabric and clip thread.

Fig. 19

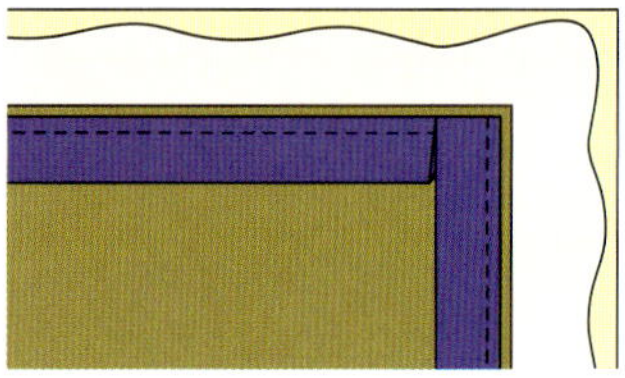

6. Continue sewing binding to quilt, stopping approximately 10" from starting point (**Fig. 20**).

Fig. 20

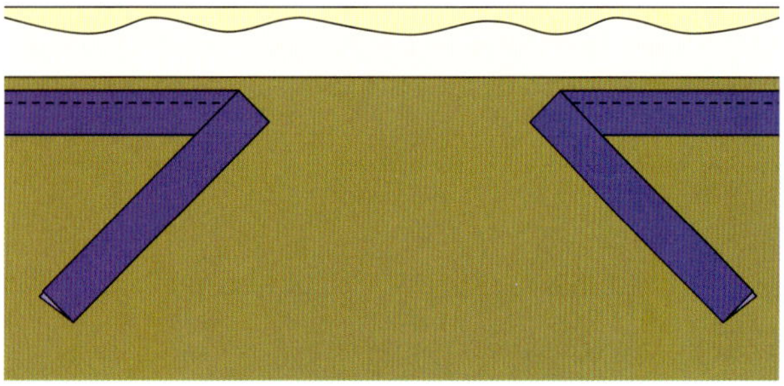

7. Bring beginning and end of binding to center of opening and fold each end back, leaving a $^{1}/_{4}$" space between folds (**Fig. 21**). Finger press folds.

Fig. 21

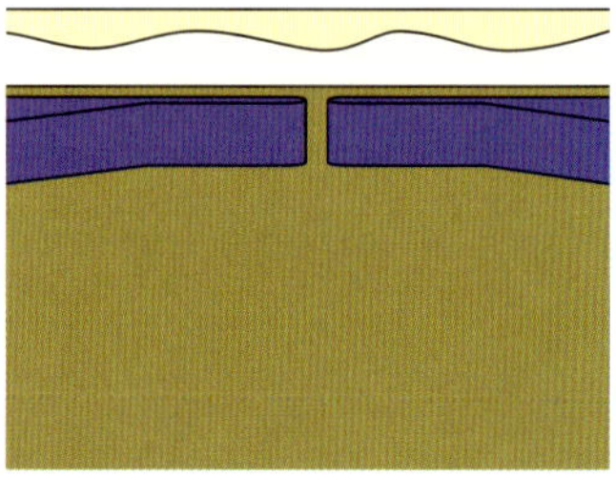

8. Unfold ends of binding and draw a line across wrong side in finger-pressed crease. Draw a line through the lengthwise pressed fold of binding at the same spot to create a cross mark. With edge of ruler at cross mark, line up 45° angle marking on ruler with one long side of binding. Draw a diagonal line from edge to edge. Repeat on remaining end, making sure that the two diagonal lines are angled the same way (**Fig. 22**).

Fig. 22

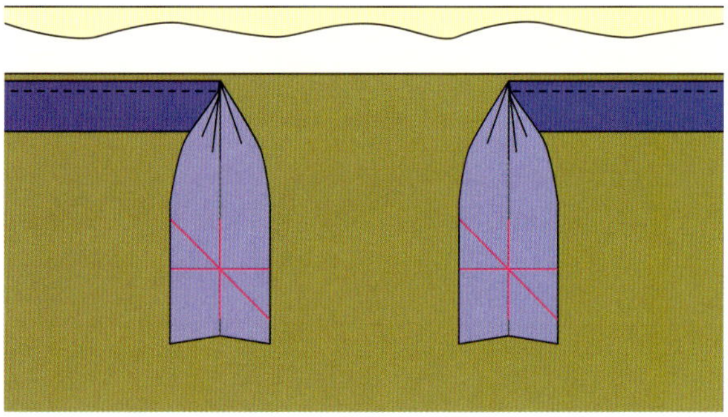

9. Matching right sides and diagonal lines, pin binding ends together at right angles (**Fig. 23**).

Fig. 23

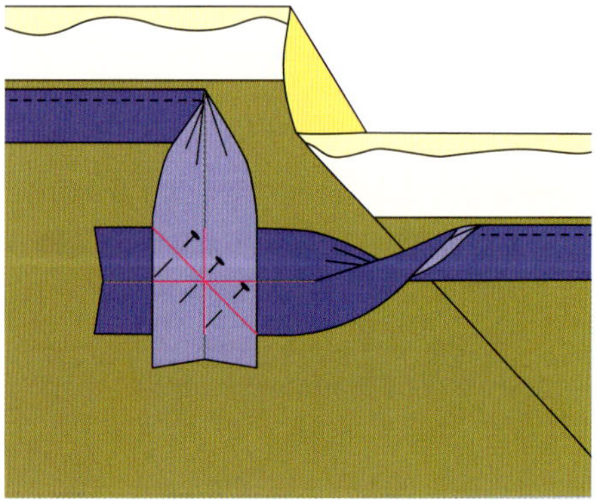

10. Machine stitch along diagonal line **(Fig. 24)**, removing pins as you stitch.

Fig. 24

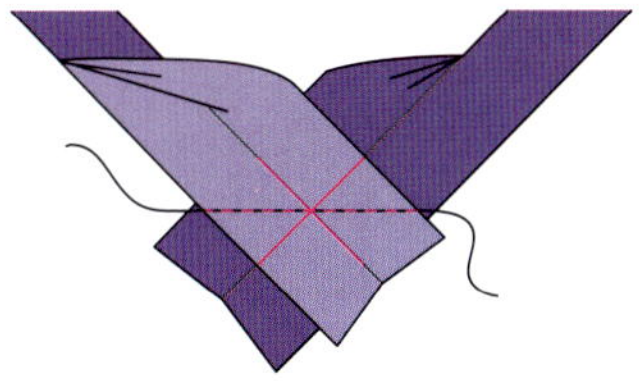

11. Lay binding against quilt to double check that it is correct length.
12. Trim binding ends, leaving a 1/4" seam allowance; press seam open. Stitch binding to quilt.
13. Trim backing and batting even with edges of quilt top.
14. On one edge of quilt, fold binding over to quilt backing and pin pressed edge in place, covering stitching line **(Fig. 25)**. On adjacent side, fold binding over, forming a mitered corner **(Fig. 26)**. Repeat to pin remainder of binding in place.

Fig. 25

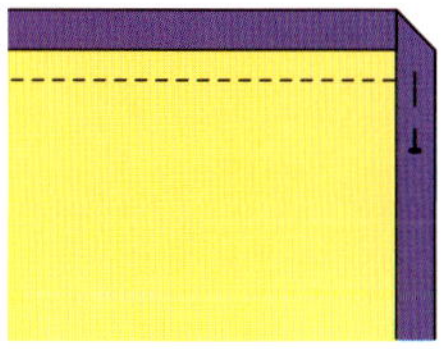

Fig. 26

15. Blindstitch binding to backing, taking care not to stitch through to front of quilt.

BLIND STITCH

Come up at 1, go down at 2, and come up at 3 **(Fig. 27)**. Length of stitches may be varied as desired.

Fig. 27

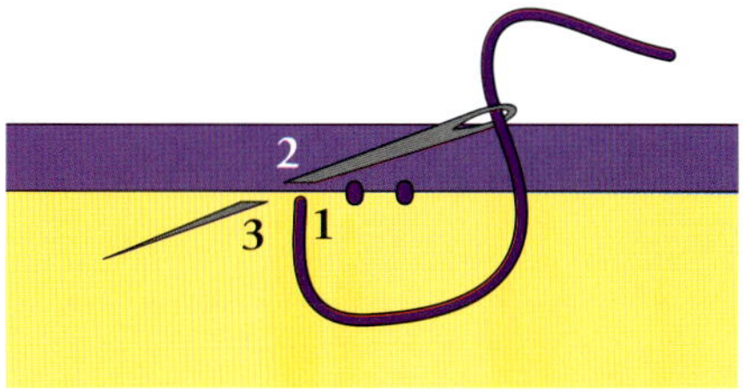

Signing and Dating Your Quilt

A completed quilt is a work of art and should be signed and dated. There are many different ways to do this and numerous books on the subject. The label should reflect the style of the quilt, the occasion or person for which it was made, and the quilter's own particular talents. Following are suggestions for recording the history of quilt or adding a sentiment for future generations.

- Embroider quilter's name, date, and any additional information on quilt top or backing. Matching floss, such as cream floss on white border, will leave a subtle record. Bright or contrasting floss will make the information stand out.

- Make label from muslin and use permanent marker to write information. Use different colored permanent markers to make label more decorative. Stitch label to back of quilt.

- Use photo-transfer paper to add image to white or cream fabric label. Stitch label to back of quilt.

- Piece an extra block from quilt top pattern to use as label. Add information with permanent fabric pen. Appliqué block to back of quilt.

Caring For Your Quilt

- Wash finished quilt in cold water on gentle cycle with mild soap. Soaps such as Orvus® Paste or Charlie's Soap®, which have no softeners, fragrances, whiteners, or other additives are safest. Rinse twice in cold water.
- Use a dye magnet such as Shout® Color Catcher® each time quilt is washed to absorb any dyes that bled. When washing a quilt for the first time, you may chose to use two dye magnets for extra caution.
- Dry quilt on low heat/air fluff in 15 minute increments until dry.

Production Team

Technical Editor – Lisa Lancaster
Technical Writer – Jean Lewis
Editorial Writer – Susan McManus Johnson
Lead Graphic Artist – Amy Temple
Graphic Artist – Jacob Casleton
Photography Stylist – Sondra Daniel
Photographer – Ken West

Metric Conversion Chart

Inches x 2.54 = centimeters (cm)	Yards x .9144 = meters (m)
Inches x 25.4 = millimeters (mm)	Yards x 91.44 = centimeters (cm)
Inches x .0254 = meters (m)	Centimeters x .3937 = inches (")
	Meters x 1.0936 = yards (yd)

Standard Equivalents

1/8"	3.2 mm	0.32 cm	1/8 yard	11.43 cm	0.11 m
1/4"	6.35 mm	0.635 cm	1/4 yard	22.86 cm	0.23 m
3/8"	9.5 mm	0.95 cm	3/8 yard	34.29 cm	0.34 m
1/2"	12.7 mm	1.27 cm	1/2 yard	45.72 cm	0.46 m
5/8"	15.9 mm	1.59 cm	5/8 yard	57.15 cm	0.57 m
3/4"	19.1 mm	1.91 cm	3/4 yard	68.58 cm	0.69 m
7/8"	22.2 mm	2.22 cm	7/8 yard	80 cm	0.8 m
1"	25.4 mm	2.54 cm	1 yard	91.44 cm	0.91 m